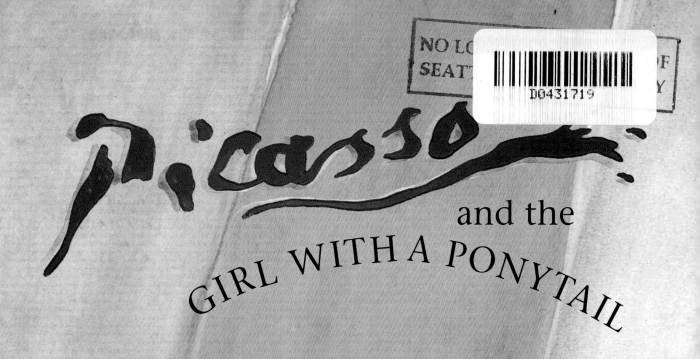

Picasso

and the
GIRL WITH A PONYTAIL

A Story about **Pablo Picasso**

by LAURENCE
ANHOLT

IT WAS THE FIRST DAY OF SUMMER. Sylvette and her friends were sitting on the terrace in the sun. Sylvette was so shy that she always sat a little apart, but she listened to every word.

"Have you heard? Picasso is staying right here in Vallauris!"

"It's incredible! The most famous artist in the world. Every picture he paints is worth a fortune."

"I heard he had a huge white car sent from America, in exchange for just one painting!"

Sylvette was very interested. Secretly, she dreamed
of becoming an artist. In a suitcase under her bed was
a sketchbook full of her drawings. All her secrets
were locked inside that suitcase – things no one else
had ever seen.

Suddenly Sylvette noticed something absolutely amazing.
Right in front of her eyes, a beautiful picture had appeared
above the terrace wall.

"LOOK!" shouted her friends. "It's Sylvette. Only Sylvette
has a ponytail like that."

Sylvette hid her face in her hands.
She heard a roar of laughter from
behind the wall.

They all ran to look. They saw
a man holding the picture above
his head. He was short, but very
muscular. He wore a striped shirt,
shorts, and a pair of bedroom
slippers. It was Picasso!

"I saw you all from my studio,"
he laughed. "And I made a sketch.
Come on. Why don't you visit me?"

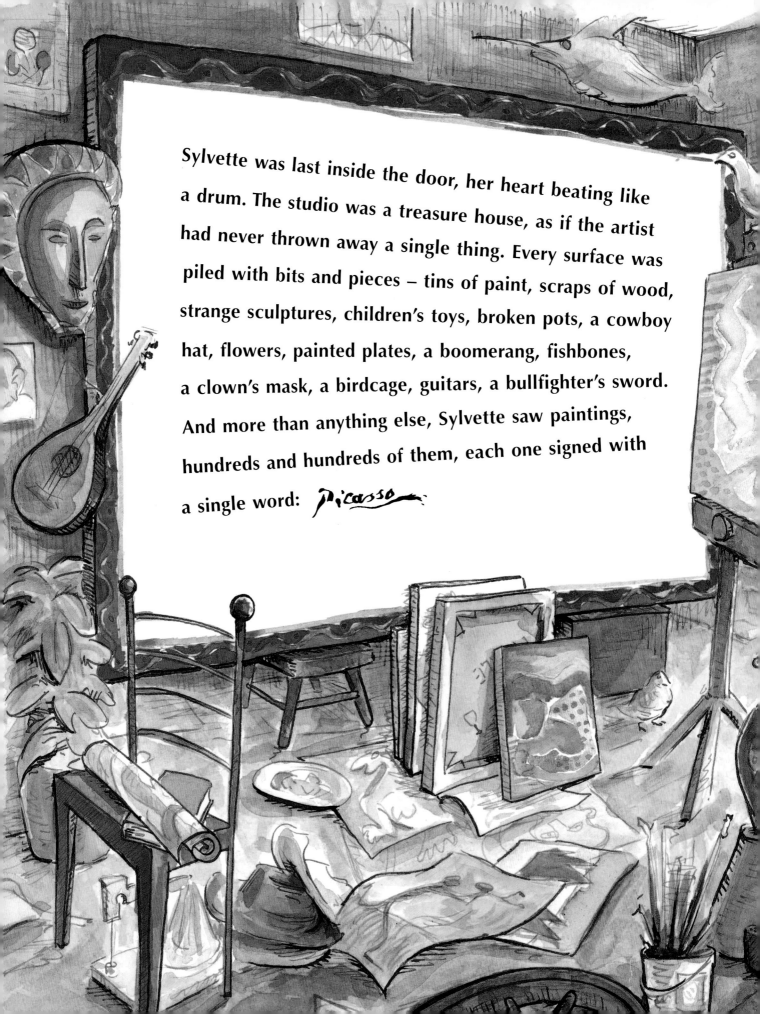

Sylvette was last inside the door, her heart beating like a drum. The studio was a treasure house, as if the artist had never thrown away a single thing. Every surface was piled with bits and pieces – tins of paint, scraps of wood, strange sculptures, children's toys, broken pots, a cowboy hat, flowers, painted plates, a boomerang, fishbones, a clown's mask, a birdcage, guitars, a bullfighter's sword. And more than anything else, Sylvette saw paintings, hundreds and hundreds of them, each one signed with a single word: *Picasso*

Picasso was still laughing. He was 73 years old, but he acted like a young boy.

"Now then," he shouted. "I will draw one person. Who will it be?"

One of Sylvette's friends stepped forward quickly. She was very beautiful. "You can draw me, Mr. Picasso," she said. "I will sit for you."

Picasso looked at her quite fiercely. "No," he said. "You saw my picture outside. I have chosen the girl with the ponytail."

Sylvette felt a bit sick. She wanted to run straight out of the door. But Picasso was very kind. "It's all right," he said gently. "You can trust me. Come and sit down."

"Sylvette is too shy," teased her friends, "and too dreamy as well."

"That's good," laughed the artist.
"Then we will get along. Because Picasso
is a dreamer, too. Come back another
time," he called to Sylvette's friends.
"Sylvette and I have work to do."

Picasso looked carefully at Sylvette.
She was shivering.

"Here, borrow this coat," he said.

Then he began to draw.

The first drawing was slow and careful – a delicate pencil study.

The second picture was larger – Sylvette as still and nervous as a wild deer.

Then Picasso began to work faster and faster.
The pictures grew larger and more strange.
Picasso was enjoying himself.

At the end of the day, Sylvette ran home. She took out her sketchbook, but her head was spinning, and none of her drawings came out right.

The next morning, Sylvette returned nervously to the studio. Perhaps Picasso had forgotten her? But he opened the door and grinned at her like a schoolboy.

Little by little, the paintings became more daring and more extraordinary. Little by little, Sylvette became less shy.

Picasso seemed to change every moment, just like his pictures. He was as proud as a king, he painted like a magician, and yet he liked to dress up and play games. Sometimes he put on funny hats or masks to make Sylvette laugh. He told her about the animals he had owned – dogs, a goat who was allowed to sleep indoors, and a bad-tempered monkey. Once he had even kept an owl. Of course, Picasso had painted them all.

All through the summer, Picasso created pictures of Sylvette, and sculptures in cardboard and metal. As the work became bigger and bolder, she became braver, too. Sylvette's father had left home when she was small, but for that summer, Picasso was like a father to her.

Shy Sylvette with the most famous painter in the world. It was a real fairy tale.

One day, Sylvette plucked up her courage and showed Picasso her secret sketchbook. She told him about her dream of becoming an artist. Picasso didn't laugh or tease her.

"That is good," he said loudly. "But you have to be brave and learn to let go. Look at me!

When I am angry,
I make angry pictures.

When I am sad,
my pictures are sad, too,

and when I am happy,
my painting is full of joy.
Even my dreams are in
my work. There can be
no secrets in painting."

That afternoon a photographer came to the
studio. Sylvette hated having her photo taken.
She wanted to hide away. Then she saw
Picasso making funny faces at the camera,
and suddenly it didn't seem so bad.
The man took dozens of pictures of
Picasso and Sylvette beside the paintings.

Her friends couldn't believe their eyes. Shy Sylvette on the front cover of a famous magazine! And before long, every magazine wanted a picture of Picasso's new model. Girls in Paris and London were even copying her hairstyle – they all wanted a Sylvette ponytail!

Sylvette cut out all the photographs and locked them carefully in her suitcase.

Sometimes Picasso worked late into the night. Once Sylvette saw him behind the studio, in the middle of a pile of garbage, hunting for interesting objects . . . The richest artist who ever lived made sculptures from old junk.

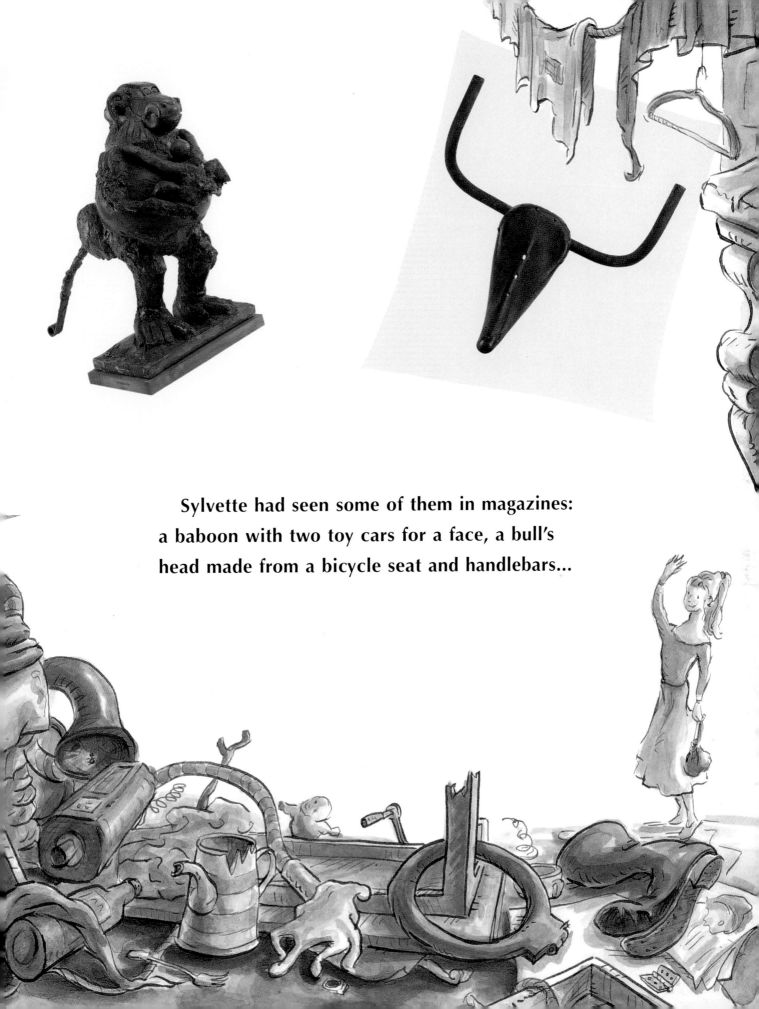

Sylvette had seen some of them in magazines:
a baboon with two toy cars for a face, a bull's
head made from a bicycle seat and handlebars...

Sylvette loved watching Picasso work.
Paintings, sculptures, and painted pots poured
from him like a volcano.

At last Picasso started a huge sculpture of Sylvette, with old
pieces of pottery for the arms and legs. It had a long neck
and a round bag just like hers, but the head was so strange,
Sylvette didn't think it looked like her at all.

    As she watched, Sylvette had a sad feeling that this would
    be the last time Picasso would use her as his model.
    Since the day on the terrace, she had been in his work.
    Soon it would all fade like the summer.

While Picasso worked, Sylvette began telling him her secrets. She talked about the time her father had gone away. Sylvette kept a special picture of him in her suitcase, but she had never told anyone how hurt and lonely she had been.

Picasso looked up at her with burning black eyes. "It is very hard when people move apart," he said. "But try to remember – with every door that closes, a new door opens."

It began to grow dark. As they looked at the sculpture, Sylvette told Picasso a secret she had locked away and tried to forget. She talked about the man who had come to live with her mother, a loud unpleasant bully. Sylvette was sometimes so unhappy that she wanted to run away.

Picasso looked at her kindly. Then he jumped up.
"You have given me an idea," he said. "I knew something
was missing from the sculpture . . . Sylvette must hold
something in her hand!"

Picasso began searching through bits
and pieces on a table. He tipped
out a drawer onto the floor.

At last he found what he wanted.
"In her hand," Picasso announced,
"Sylvette holds . . . a key!"
He pushed a big iron key
into the hand of the sculpture.
Sylvette looked puzzled.

"She has a key because she has so many
secrets locked away." Picasso fixed the key
in place with some plaster. "But she also
has a key . . . listen, Sylvette . . . to open
new doors!"

Then Picasso reached out
his hand, white with
plaster, and gently
touched Sylvette's face.

"Look! It is finished –
The Girl with a Key.
Now, Sylvette, I would
like to give you a present.
You may choose any
picture you like. Perhaps
it will help to open some doors for you."

When Sylvette stepped out of
Picasso's studio for the last time,
she was carrying that very first picture.
She held it carefully because the paint
on the signature was not quite dry –
For Sylvette, From Picasso. A beautiful
picture of The Girl with a Ponytail.

After that summer, Sylvette began to paint as bravely as Picasso had taught her. Gradually she became a well-known artist herself.

When the picture Picasso gave her was sold, Sylvette had enough money to pay for a beautiful apartment of her very own, with space for a real studio, high on the top floor, with views across the whole of Paris.

Sylvette ran up the stairs. She turned the key – and opened the door . . .

Pablo Picasso was born in Spain in 1881, the son of an art teacher. He could draw before he could speak, and by the time he was twelve he had started to produce astonishingly skillful oil paintings. Throughout his long life his output in every medium was matched only by the extraordinary range of his styles. From delicate etchings to massive and terrifying paintings like *Guernica*, Picasso's work was always pioneering and brutally honest.

Picasso bought a house in Vallauris in the South of France. Here, in 1954, he caught sight of a beautiful, shy teenager, Sylvette David. In a typically frenzied burst of creative energy, Picasso produced more than forty images of "The Girl with a Ponytail," who became an international icon. This was a turbulent time for Picasso. He had recently separated from Françoise Gilot, and met his last wife, Jacqueline Roque, at a pottery in Vallauris. For one summer, Sylvette was Picasso's platonic muse. He always treated her with kindness and respect.

The following year, Picasso had a big exhibition of his "Sylvette" paintings in Paris. Visitors were amazed to see how the work had grown from the first delicate drawing to the sculpture of the girl with a key. But it didn't stop there. A few years later, two concrete sculptures of Sylvette, each as big as a house, were built to Picasso's designs, in Holland and New York.

Picasso produced more than 30,000 original works. He died in 1973, aged 92, one of the most famous artists in the world.

Sylvette David, now Lydia Corbett, lives and paints in the West of England. Her beautiful pictures and wood sculptures can be seen at the Francis Kyle Gallery in London.